HOME

Written by Pauline Cartwright
Illustrated by Coral Tulloch

When Mrs Watson and Cassie
looked out of their window at night,
there were lights everywhere—
flashing and flickering.
The streetlight beside their house
made a yellow pool on the road.

There were smells in the air
of car fumes and chimney smoke
and, if the day had been hot,
there was a smell of tar.

Sometimes, they could smell the food
that the people were eating,
in the Chinese restaurant across the road.

All night, as they lay in bed,
they could hear car tyres hissing on the road.
SSSsss, SSSsss, SSSsss, SSSsss
as the cars went by.
Sometimes they heard them honking.
Beep-beep! Honk-honk! Beep-beep!

Now and again, very late at night,
they heard an alley cat yowling.
Y-e-e-owl! Y-e-e-owl!

"What would it be like," said Mrs Watson,
"to sleep without all this?
What would it be like to sleep in the country
in a tent?"

So, one weekend, they went on a long journey
to the country.
They had a new red tent in the back of the car
and two warm sleeping bags.

They went fishing and Cassie caught two fish.
They cooked them for tea on a campfire.
When the dark started stealing around them,
they went to bed.

Outside their tent doorway,
there were hills and valleys
in black and purple shadow.
Above them were a thousand stars,
winking and shimmering and sparkling.

They could smell sun-soaked grasses
and the ashes of their campfire.
Now and again, the scent of flowers
drifted into their dreams.

They could hear the trickle of river water,
and the rustle of leaves when the trees
moved in a passing breeze.
Now and again, a night bird called.

In the morning, Mrs Watson and Cassie drove back towards the city because, next day, Mrs Watson had to go to work and Cassie had to go to school.

By nightfall, they were back with the city lights.
The air was full of city smells
and loud with city sounds.

“I did like the country,” sighed Cassie.

“So did I,” said Mrs Watson.

“But all the same,” said Cassie,
“I’m used to this. It feels like home.”

“It is home,” said Mrs Watson.

They unpacked the car,
then they climbed into bed.
"I can smell fried rice," said Cassie.

"Listen to that cat," said Mrs Watson.
"He's out early."

While the lights flashed and flickered
and the car tyres hissed in the busy street,
Mrs Watson and Cassie drifted off to sleep.